Fast in a Jam

by Quentin Roberts
illustrated by Stephen Ochoa

Practice Decodable 8

Mc Graw Hill Education

Bothell, WA • Chicago, IL • Columbus, OH • New York, NY

MHEonline.com

Send all inquiries to:
McGraw-Hill Education
8787 Orion Place
Columbus, OH 43240

ISBN: 978-0-02-145042-8
MHID: 0-02-145042-0

Printed in the United States of America.

8 9 10 CTM 23

A jam stops a cab.

A jam is not for Jim.

The cab is not for Jim.

Jim is fit and fast.

Jim can jog past a jam.

The cab sits in a jam.